COPING WITH
RACIAL
INEQUALITY

Tamra B. Orr

Rosen
YA

New York

Published in 2018 by The Rosen Publishing Group, Inc.
29 East 21st Street, New York, NY 10010

First Edition

Library of Congress Cataloging-in-Publication Data

Names: Orr, Tamra, author.
Title: Coping with racial inequality / Tamra B. Orr.
Description: First edition. | New York NY : Rosen Publishing, [2018] |
 Series: Coping | Includes bibliographical references and index. |
 Audience: Grades 7–12.
Identifiers: LCCN 2017001578 | ISBN 9781508173960 (library bound book)
Subjects: LCSH: Racism—United States—Juvenile literature. | Race
 Discrimination—Prevention—Juvenile literature. | Race
 discrimination—Psychological aspects—Juvenile literature. | United
 States—Race relations—Anecdotes—Juvenile literature. |
 Anti-racism—United States—Juvenile literature. | Social action—United
 States—Handbooks, manuals, etc. | Teenagers—Political activity—United
 States. | Self-help techniques.
Classification: LCC E184.A1 O78 2018 | DDC 305.800973—dc23
LC record available at https://lccn.loc.gov/2017001578

Manufactured in the United States of America

CONTENTS

INTRODUCTION

It was Caro's sixteenth birthday and she had big plans. She and six of her girlfriends had coordinated what they were wearing to school that day—everyone wore shades of pink and maroon. Then it happened. "All of us were accused by our school's assistant principal of being in a Mexican gang," Caro explained years later in an interview with the author. "They thought we were wearing our gang colors to school."

Without parental permission or the students' knowledge, photographs of the girls were passed to the gang task force of the Austin, Texas, police department. "We were expelled and our parents were called to come and pick us up," Caro said. None of the students were given a chance to explain or defend themselves. Caro and her friends were Latinas of mostly Mexican heritage attending a primarily white high school.

"After a few outraged parents showed up defending their daughters, our punishment was changed to a suspension," Caro explained. All of the girls felt they were specifically targeted because they were Mexican. "I remember an abundance of outrage and disbelief that the school administrators would go so far as to expel innocent kids," she added. "I was fortunate that I had parents who believed in me, who knew me, who defended me and stood up against such an intimidating force."

Even though the girls' punishments was reduced, Caro "felt so disgusted and humiliated that [she] decided not to return to that school ever again." She further explained, "I was never ashamed of my Mexican heritage but [I was] angry that, as Latinos, we had been mistreated and falsely accused because of our ethnicity." While the rest of her friends returned to the school, Caro went to an alternative high school. She worked hard and graduated at 16 years old with a perfect 4.0 grade average. The American Civil Liberties Union (ACLU) stepped in when some of the families sued the Austin Independent School District, and the case was settled out of court.

Caro went to college and graduated as valedictorian with an associate's degree. She participated in the Oregon Council for Hispanic Advancement through the Oregon Leadership Institute. Caro chose to homeschool her daughter, in part because of the incident, and hopes to become a stronger, better advocate for people like herself and her friends.

Being treated differently—or negatively—because of one's race is nothing new in the United

States. For centuries, here and abroad, many people have been mistreated and misunderstood simply because they had a different shade of skin, or wore

This illustration of an 1830s slave auction is just one reminder of the ongoing racial injustice and intolerance throughout the nation's history.

different clothing. Despite legislation and slowly changing attitudes, many are still bullied, attacked, or vilified.

Unfortunately, no single organization, idea, or movement, let alone book, is enough to address racial inequality. Hopefully, you will learn to recognize inequality whenever it is occurring; find methods for coping if it is happening to you or someone around you; and finally, discover ways of making your life and the lives of those you care about better by making positive changes.

CHAPTER ONE

A History of Race in America

The world has changed greatly over the past several centuries. If you transported a few people from the eighteenth century to the modern world, they would most likely be shocked and overwhelmed by the changes. Seeing automobiles, huge skyscrapers, and various forms of twentieth- and twenty-first-century technologies, they would assume they were having a strange dream of some kind. It truly would be an alien world to them because of the vast advances humans have made.

Unfortunately, one serious issue has persisted for centuries: racial inequality. In particular, the United States, Canada, and many other nations have fallen woefully short of guaranteeing and providing the equal rights they promise. Much progress has been made, but many of the systems that prop up inequality have merely changed shape.

Europeans first conquered the Western hemisphere at the expense of its native inhabitants. Unlike the rapid progress of technology, medicine, and other man-made phenomena, the efforts to reform our social systems and eliminate inequality have been far slower and more complicated. To understand why today's world has a problem with racial inequality, it is essential to recall yesterday's battles for civil rights and self-determination.

Losing their Land

History is endlessly full of stories of brave and adventurous explorers heading out into the unknown to discover new lands. Those stories often portray these men as heroes, and in many ways, they were. They risked their lives in order to see what really existed across the distant ocean, around the next bend in a river, or on the other side of a mountain range. It is easy to imagine that many of the lands these explorers found were unpopulated and waiting to be discovered. Instead they were often home to various indigenous populations. In the conflicts that erupted between these people and European explorers and conquerors, the indigenous people were either killed or mistreated. Many fought back, but they were eventually beaten by the Europeans' superior military might, or by European diseases that ravaged their populations.

A chief of the Ute people stands before Chimney Rock, in Ute National Park in Colorado. The Ute are one of many indigenous tribes displaced by European settlers since the nation's founding.

Beginning in the fifteenth century, around the same time Europeans first conquered parts of the Americas, blacks from different regions of Africa were captured to be sold as slaves. Over the next five centuries, millions of Africans were captured. They were put on ships and shipped in inhumane conditions to the newly settled American colonies, including modern day United States, Cuba, Haiti, and Brazil, as well as some European countries.

After establishing the original Thirteen Colonies of the United States, the population of this newly formed country began to push westward. Thousands—likely even millions—of Native Americans became casualties of this expansion. In the nineteenth century, after a period of conflict, a treaty between the United

States and Mexico (the Treaty of Guadalupe-Hidalgo) resulted in Mexico losing all of the territories making up modern-day Arizona, Texas, California, New Mexico, and Colorado, as well as parts of Utah and Nevada. In the century following, both the indigenous peoples of these lands, and the Mexican-Americans that lived and settled there as immigrants were often disenfranchised, or denied access to jobs and services available to other settlers and stripped of their civil rights and human dignity.

New Battle, Old Battle

In the fall of 2016 the world was riveted by a showdown in North Dakota that eerily echoed the battles our nation saw more than a century ago. Once again, Native Americans were put into a position of protecting their land, no matter how long it took or what the final cost might be.

The Texas-based Energy Transfer Partners wanted to build a 1,172-mile pipeline to carry 570,000 barrels of oil each day from North Dakota to Illinois. They ran into a big problem, however: Native American tribes objected. The pipeline would run underneath the Missouri River, which provides the main drinking water for the 10,000 people living on the Standing Rock Sioux reservation. The Sioux worried a leak could contaminate their water supplies. In addition, the pipeline would run through a sacred burial ground.

In the beginning, the protests came from the Sioux, but over time, more and more people joined the debate. Members from hundreds of different tribes came to join the battle. Thousands of other people traveled to the area to join and support the water protectors, as they are calling themselves, including celebrities Mark Ruffalo and Shailene Woodley. The protestors were closely monitored by the National Guard and police officers, and many people were arrested. The peaceful protest turned rather violent, with officers using pepper spray, rubber bullets, concussion cannons, and police dogs against unarmed protestors.

In early December, federal authorities put a stop to all construction of the Dakota Access pipeline. The Native Americans have won, for now. The US Army Corps of Engineers determined that an alternative route would have to be used. Brian Cladoosby, president of the National Congress of American Indians said in an official statement to the press, "My hands go up to all the water protectors who have stood up to protect tribal treaty rights and to protect Mother Earth."

Time for Change

Countless textbooks, memoirs, biographies, novels, and films make it clear that life as a slave was difficult and dangerous for black people. Slavery meant you were owned by someone else, and your life and fate was entirely controlled by them. Even the Constitution stated in 1789 that slaves were only considered three-fifths of a person. The issue of slavery was hotly debated and eventually led to the US Civil War (1861–1865). Abraham Lincoln's Emancipation Proclamation of 1862 declared that, as of January 1, 1863, all slaves "shall be then, thenceforward, and forever free." When it took effect, 3.1 million of the country's 4 million slaves were freed. Despite this step, it was not until April 8, 1864, that the Thirteenth Amendment became a legally binding amendment to the Constitution. It stated that:

> *"Neither slavery nor involuntary servitude, except as a punishment for crime whereof the party shall have been duly convicted, shall exist within the United States, or any place subject to their jurisdiction."*

The amendment was ratified in 1865, the same year the Civil War ended and Lincoln himself was assassinated by a pro-slavery extremist. At last, slavery was abolished. Sadly, racial inequality was not abolished, and would continue for far longer than most could have guessed.

Battles for Equality

While the most well-known struggle of the nineteenth century was African Americans' quest for freedom and equality, other fights continued simultaneously. In 1867, about 2,000 Chinese workers, who had been toiling away building the Central Pacific Railroad, went on strike. They wanted better pay and shorter hours (less than ten hours a day). In response the railroad building companies cut off their food supplies, and threatened the Chinese workers with steep fines—or violence. The strike ended unsuccessfully.

In 1882, Congress passed the Chinese Exclusion Act, the first significant law in the United States restricting immigration. Even though many Chinese came to the country to work on major construction projects, many Americans resented them. They blamed the Chinese for taking jobs from Americans, since the foreign workers were willing to work for lower wages. A wave of anti-Chinese sentiment gripped Americans— they considered the Chinese "the yellow peril." Chinese immigration was severely restricted for ten years. All Chinese people were forced to carry identification cards. Those already here were not allowed to become citizens. In 1888, the Scott Act was passed, which

Chinese immigrant laborers work on the Central Pacific Railroad in California's Sierra Nevada Mountains in 1867. Such workers were not treated as full Americans for a very long time.

stated that any Chinese laborers who left the United States for any reason could not return unless they had family here. The Chinese Exclusion Act was renewed for another ten years in 1892.

In Montana, in 1876, the Sioux and Cheyenne tribes fought federal troops at the Battle of Little Big Horn. Known as "Custer's last stand," this victory by two Native American tribes was temporary. The loss of so many soldiers only made people see Indians as primitive and dangerous, and efforts to exterminate them and steal their land intensified. Less than five years later, these Native Americans were all relocated to live on reservations. Congress did not grant citizenship to Native Americans until 1924, when they passed the Indian Citizenship Act.

In 1910, a number of Mexicans immigrated to the United States to escape the Mexican revolution. They were not welcomed. By 1912, the Mexican ambassador spoke out against the constant lynching and

Young Japanese students say the US Pledge of Allegiance in San Francisco. They were among the nearly 120,000 Japanese Americans who were detained in camps during World War II.

murder of Mexicans throughout the country. In 1930, more than 400,000 Mexicans were deported for fear they would take American jobs.

After the Japanese bombed Pearl Harbor in World War II (December 7, 1941), Japanese-Americans found themselves suspected of collaborating with the enemy. By 1942, a number of relocation or internment camps had been established in California, Idaho, Utah, Arizona, Wyoming, Colorado, and Arkansas. More than 110,000 Japanese Americans were taken there forcibly and kept detained behind chain linked fences covered in barbed wire.

New Laws

In 1868, the Fourteenth Amendment was passed, stating that African Americans were full citizens with equal protection and the right to due process under the law. This essentially meant that they had the same rights to fair and equal treatment in the judicial system as anyone else. Two years later, the Fifteenth Amendment was passed. It gave every male, regardless of race, the right to vote. (Women would not be given this right until 1920 when the Twentieth Amendment was passed).

While these amendments were certainly steps in the right direction, simply adding them to the Constitution did not change social attitudes about race or give people of color equal access to important resources. For the last 30 years of the twentieth century, a number of laws were also put into place to segregate blacks and white on trains and depots, as well as ships and wharves. Soon blacks were not allowed in hotels, restaurants, theaters, barber shops, and other public places. Schools remained completely segregated.

Even though the Fifteenth Amendment made it legal for African Americans to vote, a number of states passed poll tax laws. The poll tax was a fee each person had to pay in order to register to vote. This prevented many poor people from exercising their right to vote. After centuries of slavery and unequal pay, most black citizens lived in poverty. In addition, many states imposed literacy tests: each voter had to prove he or she could read, but poll officials usually decided how many questions to ask and if the answers were correct. Many officials picked and chose who had to take these tests, and often worked behind the scenes to make sure non-white voters failed them.

In 1896, in the landmark case of *Plessy v Ferguson*, the US Supreme Court determined that keeping the races separate was legal as long as the races had "equal accommodations." This was also known as the "separate but equal" doctrine. The case grew out of an 1892 incident when passenger Homer Plessy refused to sit in the blacks only train car in Louisiana.

Segregated facilities for blacks, however, were never equal to those of whites. The decision was overturned in 1954 with *Brown v Board of Education*. The Supreme Court ruled that segregating the races was illegal and unconstitutional. In 1957, the first group of African American students, known as the Little Rock Nine, enrolled at Central High School in Little Rock, Arkansas. Despite the Supreme Court's ruling, the students had to be escorted by federal troops to protect them from the mobs protesting their enrollment.

Civil Disobedience

Rosa Parks had had a long day on December 1, 1955. She wanted to sit down. She took a seat on a Montgomery, Alabama bus. She did not realize she was about to change the world. When a white man asked Parks to give him her seat, she refused. The bus driver demanded that she move, but she still said no.

From the Icons

Some of history's most important icons have held forth eloquently on the problem of racial inequality:

"Racism is still with us. But it is up to us to prepare our children for what they have to meet, and hopefully, we shall overcome." ~Rosa Parks

"I have a dream that my four little children will one day live in a nation where they will not be judged by the color of their skin, but by the content of their character." ~*Martin Luther King, Jr.*

"If we cannot end our differences, at least we can help make the world safe for diversity." ~ *John F. Kennedy*

"The earth is the mother of all people, and all people should have equal rights upon it." ~ *Chief Joseph*

"Change will not come if we wait for some other person or some other time. We are the ones we've been waiting for. We are the change that we seek." ~*Barack Obama*

It wasn't because she was tired from work. Later she would write in her autobiography, "No, the only tired I was, was tired of giving in."

She was arrested for not cooperating. Her arrest soon inspired civil rights leader Martin Luther King Jr. to organize an official bus boycott throughout Montgomery. According to the King Center, they handed out leaflets saying, "Don't ride the bus to work, to town, to school, or any place Monday, December 5. Another Negro Woman has been arrested and put in jail because she refused to give up her bus seat . . . If you work, take a cab, or share a ride, or walk."

As a result, about 99 percent of African Americans in the city did not ride the bus. Carpools were organized. The bus company was soon under financial pressure. On November 23, 1956, less than a year later, the Supreme Court stated that segregated bus seating was unconstitutional. Fifty years later, on December 5, 2005, transit authorities in New York City, Washington, DC, and other major cities left the seat behind bus driver empty to honor Rosa Parks and her important act of civil disobedience.

The 1960s were a time of huge change for African Americans and other minorities. In 1960, lunch counter sit-ins began in Greensboro, North Carolina, and spread across the South. The following year, Freedom Rides were launched on Greyhound buses traveling through southern states. A group of 13 African-American and white activists

Protesters march in Marion, Alabama, in February 1965, during one of many actions during the famous Selma to Montgomery marches in which blacks and their allies demanded civil rights.

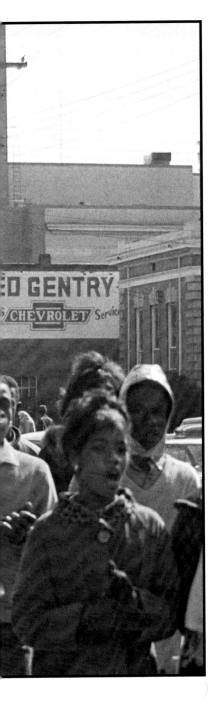

left from Washington, DC and traveled on buses to integrate bus stations, restrooms, and waiting rooms. As they traveled, other volunteers joined the cause. Some of the riders were beaten and their buses chased and bombed on the road. The National Guard was brought in to restore order.

In August 1963, Martin Luther King, Jr., the face of civil rights for many people, gave his famous "I Have a Dream" speech following the march on Washington. A quarter of a million people participated in this march. It was the first of several large but peaceful marches King and his supporters would undertake. The next year, the Civil Rights Act of 1964 was passed, banning discrimination in public places and in employment. This was followed by the

Voting Rights Act of 1965 making poll taxes and literacy tests illegal and the Civil Rights Act of 1968 prohibiting discrimination by renters or people selling property. The same year, King was assassinated in Memphis. The nation mourned the loss of this advocate for racial equality.

Many historians believe that the era of civil rights ended when Martin Luther King Jr. was killed. Look up civil rights timelines online and almost all of them end with his death. In truth, civil rights and the drive to treat everyone equally despite the color of their skin or where they came from is ongoing. We may have come far since slaves were put on boats, Native Americans were killed defending their land, and immigrants were imprisoned and deported en masse, but one glance at many of today's headlines is enough to remind us all that we still have a long way to go.

Getting Under Your Skin: Race Today

When Michael Luo, Deputy Metro Editor at the *New York Times*, left church and headed out to lunch with his family, the last thing he expected was to run into racial intolerance. Suddenly, a woman down the block yelled, "Go back to China!" at him, his wife, and their small children. Luo's parents are from mainland China, but he was born in the United States. He was appalled and decided to confront the woman, but it did not help. She just kept yelling at him.

In response, he wrote an open letter to the woman and it was published in the *New York Times*. "This was not my first encounter, of course, with racist insults," he wrote. "Ask any Asian-American, and they'll readily summon memories of schoolyard taunts, or disturbing encounters on the street or at the grocery store." Luo added that, while racial insults were not new to him, this time it felt different. "Maybe you don't know this," he continued, "but the insults you hurled at my family get to the heart of the Asian-American experience. It's this persistent sense of otherness that a lot of us struggle with every day. That no matter what we do, how successful we are, what friends we make, we don't belong. We're foreign. We're not American."

Although the country has passed laws and ratified amendments to try and guarantee that all racial groups are treated fairly and equally, the harsh truth is not all Americans are sympathetic to the cause of equality. A quick look at the headlines is enough to see that discrimination and inequality are still a big problem

Many businesses have consciously made the effort to promote diverse workplaces. However, there are many industries where discrimination against minorities continues.

for Americans. One of the most concerning issues is the widespread belief that the nation's police forces apply different standards to white and non-white people—especially African Americans.

Horrid Headlines

For years, the headlines have been full of stories of police officers, security officers, and other members of law enforcment, and other authority figures, abusing and even killing young people of color. Many people have been appalled and saddened by what happened to young men like Oscar Grant, Trayvon Martin, and Michael Brown. They also lament cases like that of Sandra Bland, who died in a jail cell under mysterious circumstances after being pulled over for a minor traffic violation. These stories have undermined people's confidence in both police protection and the judicial system. Each day, many are further discouraged by new stories like these.

In June 2015, when Deputy Ben Fields was called to Robert Long's math class at Spring Valley High School in South Carolina, he had little idea of what was about to happen. A young black teenage student had violated the rules, using a cell phone in class. She refused to hand over her phone to the teacher, or to get out of her seat and go to the principal's office when told. In response, the 34-year-old white deputy (also

Black Lives Matter

In 2012, following the death of Trayvon Martin and the acquittal of his shooter, George Zimmerman, the organization *Black Lives Matter* (blacklivesmatter.com) was created by three political activists and community organizers: Alicia Garza, Patrisse Cullors, and Opal Tometi. Unlike many similar organizations, *Black Lives Matter* (BLM) focused on the local level, instead of the national. It is made up of many local, independent chapters. In an article for *USA Today*, the group states that their primary mission is to "push for black people's right to live with dignity and respect" and respond positively and effectively to anti-black racism.

President Obama has been supportive of BLM. He invited prominent activist Deray McKesson to speak about race at the White House, and, according to PJ Media, told BLM activists that they have done "outstanding work" and have "made history." Congressman Keith Ellison from Minnesota wrote, in the foreword to *Black Lives Matter* by Sue Bradford Edwards and Duchess Harris, "#BlackLivesMatter is a call to action. It's a challenge to the criminal justice system. But most of all, it's a declaration of dignity."

(continued on the next page)

(continued from the previous page)

While the movement's intentions are good, the actions of some of their members have been quite controversial. When law enforcement officer Darren Wilson was exonerated for shooting unarmed teenager Michael Brown in 2015, for example, some BLM members set the city of Ferguson, Missouri, on fire. In addition, a few members have encouraged blacks to murder any white police officers if they feel threatened or falsely accused of any wrongdoing.

the school's football coach), grabbed the student by her neck, flipped her backward, dragged her across the floor, and finally handcuffed her.

This incident was caught on multiple cell phones and circulated among news outlets and social media. Fields was fired by the sheriff's department. The FBI and Justice Department were also called in. Ultimately, no charges were filed against Fields, as prosecutors declared "no probable cause" to charge the former deputy.

In April 2016, San Antonio sixth grader Janissa Valdez was upset. She and another student were angry with each other. Valdez met her outside Rhodes Middle School to discuss it. Other students gathered around to see if the two would start to fight. Officer

Joshua Kehm, the school's 27-year-old Caucasian police officer, approached too. He misunderstood what he saw, believing that Valdez was going to initiate a fight. He grabbed the 12-year-old girl and body slammed her into the brick pavement. There was a loud crack as her head hit, and one student called out, "Janissa! Janissa, you okay? She landed on her face!"

Valdez was handcuffed, pulled to her feet, and taken away, but not before the entire incident was recorded. It did not take long for it to be released on YouTube and other social media. That was when school officials found out about the incident. A formal investigation by both the district police and the school administration was started immediately. Opinions about how the situation was handled have differed within the community. Some supported Officer Kehm's actions. Most people did not, however, especially as the officer's report on the incident was delayed and inaccurate. Judith Browne Dianis, co-director of the Advancement Project (a civil rights organization) told the *Washington Post*, "It is unconscionable for a 12-year-old student involved in a verbal altercation to be brutalized and dehumanized in this manner. Once again, a video captured by a student offers a sobering reminder that we cannot entrust school police officers to intervene in school disciplinary matters that are best suited for

Feeling that one is treated differently than one's peers, especially at school, where someone is supposed to feel welcome and safe, can be emotionally exhausting.

trained educators and counselors. How many students of color must be brutalized by police officers in their schools before we recognize the pattern?"

Because of this unwarranted use of force and his failure to report it to the district, Officer Kehm was given the opportunity either to resign or be fired. He refused to resign, so was terminated by the school district.

Negative Numbers

The stories don't end there. Across the country, in schools, workplaces, and other public places, people of all ages are suffering from some type of discrimination and mistreatment. It starts very early, with some reports stating that children of color in pre-Kindergarten, only four or five years old, are already being treated unequally.

A 2014 US Department of Education's Office for Civil Rights study found that black, Latino, and Native American students have less access to advanced math and science classes, as the schools in these communities are far less likely to offer classes in algebra and geometry or physics and chemistry. The same study reported that Native American and black students are suspended and expelled far more often than white students, for comparable offenses.

Suspensions and expulsions are especially high for girls of color. The Stand Against Racism organization states that black girls are suspended at 12 percent higher rates than girls of other races. American Indian and Alaska Native girls and Latinas are also suspended at higher rates than white girls. Being suspended from school, especially more than once, is connected to future problems like dropping out of school, having encounters with the juvenile justice system, and higher risks of low-wage work and unemployment.

Driving While Black and Other "Offenses"

Outside of school, racial conflicts and inequality are still huge problems. Driving While Black, or DWB, has become a well known peril on the nation's roads. According to the Justice Department, a black driver is 31 percent more likely to be pulled over than a

Stand Your Ground

Approximately half of the states in the United States currently have a "Stand your Ground" law in place. Florida was the first one to pass the law in 2005, and other states have followed. According to legal dictionaries, a stand your ground law means that "under certain circumstances, individuals can use force to defend themselves without first attempting to retreat from the danger." Instead of being expected to run away from danger, this law allows people to defend themselves against a perceived threat. If you are armed and you feel threatened, in other words, you have the right to protect yourself, even if it means killing the other person. As the encounter between Trayvon Martin and George Zimmerman pointed out, however, the perception of danger can be awfully vague and even completely misconstrued. For example, racial stereotypes about a person of color's attitude, actions, speech, and clothing may sometimes create fear in others. This can lead to misunderstanding—and tragedy.

white driver. Hispanic drivers are more likely than Caucasians, and Native Americans are the most likely to be pulled over of all the races. The number

Considering traffic and other annoyances, driving is bad enough without the added worry that law enforcement may racially profile you on the road.

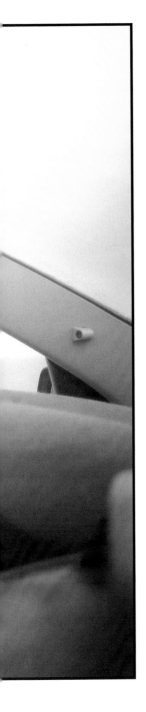

one reason for any driver to get pulled over is speeding. While 2.6 percent of Caucasian drivers are not told why they have been pulled over, 4.7 percent of African-Americans are not told. Furthermore, black drivers are more than twice as likely to be searched as their white counterparts.

Recently the Driving while Black app was introduced for drivers. According to the site (dwbtheapp.com), this app provides "helpful resources for black people and everyone to improve traffic stop experiences." The app provides sections where people can learn about their legal rights, traffic stop best practices, and safety, plus the ability to instantly inform family when stopped, record and submit complaints or commendations on law enforcement, and identify legal professionals in the area.

More people of color are getting in trouble in school and behind the wheel. How does this play out in the judicial and penal systems? According to the Shadow Report to the United Nations on Racial Disparities in the United States Criminal Justice System done in 2013, this country has seven million people under some form of correctional control (as of 2011). Of those 2.2 million are in federal, state, or local prisons and jails. Many more are on probation or parole, or in halfway houses.

The report goes on to state. "Such broad statistics mask the racial disparity that pervades the US criminal justice system. Racial minorities are more likely than white Americans to be arrested; once arrested, they are more likely to be convicted; and once convicted, they are more likely to face stiff sentences. African-American males are six times more likely to be incarcerated than white males and 2.5 times more likely than Hispanic males." According to this report, if these trends continue, "one of every three black American males born today can expect to go to prison in his lifetime, as can one of every six Latino males—compared to one of every seventeen white males."

The reasons that so many people of color are arrested and jailed are debated and studied by a wide variety of organizations. Not all the reasons are directly tied to ethnicity and racism, but aspects of those seem to filter in even where they ideally should not. In the report, "Black Lives Matter: Eliminating Racial Inequity in the Criminal Justice System," author

Nazgol Ghandnoosh, PhD, writes that he believes the differences in how the races are treated boils down to four issues:

• Many justice policies that were designed to be race-neutral collide with the socioeconomic reality. Police policies created to address populations with high crime rates are disproportionately going to affect people of color. For example, drug-free school zone laws require stronger sentences for people caught selling drugs near school zones. In the majority of cities, schools are located in densely populated areas, and have a much higher percentage of POC (people of color).

• Many people, including criminal justice professionals (police, prosecutors, judges, and courtroom workgroups), are influenced by implicit racial bias. This type of bias is defined as unintentional and unconscious bias that affects a person's decisions and behaviors.

• Key portions of the criminal justice system do not have the funding they need, which negatively impacts low-income defendants, many of which are POC. For instance, most states do not allocate enough money to their indigent defense programs. These are the systems that are supposed to provide attorneys

In a system where blacks are treated unfairly, a black teenager just standing against a fence might be seen as some kind of threat, while a white one might not get the same scrutiny.

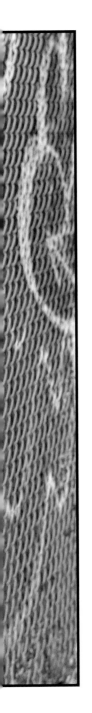

to criminal defendants who cannot otherwise afford them. Public defenders tend to be overwhelmed with high caseloads, plus have limited experience in the courtroom.

• The country's criminal justice system is primarily designed to react to crime rather than prevent it. This means it does not remedy the underlying causes. For those POC who try to reenter a community after serving time, life can be extremely difficult. It is hard to get hired with a prison record, and in many states, anyone convicted of a drug felony is not allowed to receive federal cash assistance, subsidized housing, or food stamps.

Race relations remain troubled, while racial inequality persists. How much improvement has been made and how much change is still needed depends on who you ask. In a Pew Research Center survey done in 2016, 88 percent of blacks believe more changes are needed for blacks and whites to have equal rights. Only 53 percent of whites felt that way. Just over 40 percent of blacks doubt that the country will actually be able to make these changes. Just over 10 percent of whites feel that way.

It can be encouraging for an African American person to see another while interviewing for a job, but even people in a diverse workplace can experience racial inequality or prejudice.

When Barack Obama was elected as president in 2008, many Americans hoped this would mean advancements in racial equality. As he stated in his "A More Perfect Union" speech in Philadelphia, Pennsylvania, on March 18, 2008, "This union may never be perfect, but generation after generation has shown that it can always be perfected. And today, whenever I find myself feeling doubtful or cynical about this possibility, what gives me the most hope is the next generation—the young people whose attitudes and beliefs and openness to change have already made history in this election."

Regardless of whose opinions on these issues are the most accurate, it is essential that you learn to cope effectively with any type of racial inequality in your life and find ways to make your world a better place. That is what this book is all about.

Myths & FACTS

Myth: All police officers, especially white ones, target black people on purpose.

Fact: While stories of police brutality do dominate the headlines, the idea that all police officers are specifically targeting blacks is not true.

Myth: Telling racial jokes is okay, if I am not racist myself.

Fact: Many racial jokes may seem funny, but are actually hurtful and offensive to others. You need to examine yourself and your heart to find out why you feel the need to use such humor.

Myth: Only white people have problematic attitudes on race and prejudice.

Fact: Anyone can have an attitude that other races or religions are inferior in some way. Even supposedly good people can harbor such thoughts deep inside.

Face to Face: Daily Discrimination and Personal Prejudice

Students were chattering and finding seats at Bishop Gorman School in Las Vegas, Nevada. The entire student body had gathered for a Veteran's Day assembly. Seventeen-year-old Dylan Bruton was sitting towards the back on the bleachers. He stood for the ovation and applauded.

However, when the National Anthem began to play, he decided to remain sitting down. It wasn't a premeditated decision. It just felt right. "I didn't think anyone saw me," he told KTNV News. Bruton chose not to stand for several reasons. First, he was mourning the loss of his grandfather, a veteran who had died just a few days ago. Second, he was feeling disheartened by the election of Donald Trump and the fear it inspired in people of color. Third, Bruton was showing support for

People of all ages, but young people, athletes, and youth of color especially, were inspired by the example of San Francisco 49ers quarterback Colin Kaepernick's ongoing national anthem protest.

San Francisco 49ers' player Colin Kaepernick. The quarterback had gone down on one knee during the playing of the national anthem at one of his games.

"I was very inspired by Colin Kaepernick, as a major sports fan and a young black man who is unapologetically proud of his blackness," Bruton stated in an interview with the author. In fact, one of the last things his grandfather had told Bruton was that he respected the football player and other athletes for peacefully protesting against racism. He felt more people should be doing this. "To see a prominent sports figure take a stand and fight for his people, it gives me hope. I absolutely respect, appreciate, and commend every influential black man or woman who uses their platform to uplift our people. I see myself doing the same thing moving forward in my life for my people," Bruton continued. "Whatever platform I have, I will use to uplift, empower, and educate my people."

Bruton also stated that since the 2016 presidential election, as minorities, he and his friends no longer felt safe. This was enhanced by the fact that there were political signs on school property. Students were wearing political t-shirts and hats, carrying flags, and yelling angry and offensive slurs at students of color. "They were saying things like, 'we got our country back,'" Bruton stated.

A student reported Bruton during lunch and soon Bruton was in trouble. The private Catholic school was angry with Bruton, stating his "unbecoming behavior" showed a lack of respect. "I have the utmost respect for veterans," the young man protested. "They're making a huge, huge sacrifice." He stood and applauded for the speakers' introductions and when the veterans were introduced. Bruton also took the time to shake the hands of every veteran that came to the presentation. Despite this, for not rising for the anthem, Bruton was suspended and placed on a disciplinary contract from the school. This meant that even if he broke minor school rules, he could be expelled without a hearing.

Bishop Gorman, a place Bruton called his "dream school," banned him from the football team, even though this experience did not happen anywhere near the field. The school administration also banned him from participating in the school's television broadcasts, even though they knew he wanted to become a broadcast journalist. In addition, Bruton was required to attend five sessions of counseling with student services, submit an essay on a determined topic, write a letter of apology to the veterans who attended the assembly, and participate in 70-plus hours of community service within three months.

"We did not allow Dylan to do any of the school's egregious stipulations for him to return as a full student. We withdrew him," Bruton's mother Heather said in an interview with the author. Mrs. Bruton fully supported what her son had done. "I have raised him to be confident, yet humble, a child of God, to stand for the oppressed, to help those in need," she explained. "He has been going to protests, marches, soup kitchens, and various houses of worship since he was a baby in my arms." Mrs. Bruton was proud of her son's courage. "My son became my hero that day because he said 'no more' in the most peaceful way possible."

Instead of complying with the school's discipline requirements, Bruton enrolled in a different high school. After a few weeks at the new school, he was nominated for student of the month. Bruton hopes that, by sharing his story, he will inspire people at Bishop Gorman to think. "Our family believes in racial justice and equality and, as a stage 4 cancer survivor, I believe racism is the worst cancer of the twenty-first century," adds Dylan's mother. "As I tell my children, when we truly embrace the rich, beautiful diversity of our country and honor the benefits of those differences, we will be a stronger, more compassionate, better society."

The Kaepernick Effect

Bruton explained that part of the reason he chose to sit through the national anthem was to support San Francisco 49ers' quarterback Colin Kaepernick and his efforts to bring public awareness to the problem of

Even many African American people who served in the armed forces and law enforcement agree that we have a long way to go as a nation before everyone enjoys complete equality.

racial oppression. He started by sitting during the song in preseason games, and quickly was both praised and criticized for his actions. "I am not going to stand up to show pride in a flag for a country that oppresses black people and people of color," he stated to the NFL. "To me, this is bigger than football and it would be selfish on my part to look the other way."

Many people called him unpatriotic, but he quickly denied that motive. He met with Nate Boyer, former Green Beret and Seattle Seahawks player. According to *ESPN*, the first thing Kaepernick said was, "I want you to know, first and foremost, I really do respect the heck out of the military, and I really want to thank you for your service." The 49er's quarterback wanted to keep pushing his message, but not show any disrespect to others. Sitting was seen as rude, but bowing their heads did not seem like a strong enough message.

Fellow team member Eric Reid suggested that Kaepernick kneel on one knee. Boyer agreed. "It's a good step, and it shows progress on your part and sensitivity and that you care about other people and how this affects them, their reaction,'" he added. "It's still definitely a symbol. People take a knee to pray. In the military, we take a knee all the time. It's one of the things we do. When we're exhausted on patrol, they say take a knee and face out. So we take a knee like that. We'll take a knee as the classic symbol of respect in front of a brother's grave site, a soldier on a knee."

Since Kaepernick decided to kneel during "The Star Spangled Banner," many professional sports players have done the same. Each week, more and more players have gone to one knee. Others have joined hands, linked arms, or raised fists to display their feelings. Players from more than a dozen NFL teams have participated, as well as WNBA (Women's National Basketball Association) players, soccer players, tennis players, and swimmers. Even some of the national anthem singers are performing on one knee.

The professional sports teams are not the only ones deciding to kneel. As of early November 2016, fifty-two high schools, thirty-nine colleges, one middle school, and two youth leagues have also chosen to kneel during the song. While many applaud this nonviolent method of protesting, others are incensed by it. Students and coaches are kneeling, and so are cheerleaders, and pep band members.

While Kaepernick did not expect such a response to his actions, he is pleased to see how it has spread. As he told the NFL, "This stand wasn't for me. This is because I'm seeing things happen to people that don't have a voice, people that don't have a platform to talk and have their voices heard, and effect change. So I'm in the position where I can do that and I'm going to

A protester holds a sign referencing the last words of Eric Garner, a 43-year-old father who died from a police chokehold in 2014. Video of Garner's death went viral, sparking debates on police brutality.

do that for people that can't . . . It's something that can unify this team. It's something that can unify this country. If we have these real conversations that are uncomfortable for a lot of people. If we have these conversations, there's a better understanding of where both sides are coming from."

University of Michigan linebacker Mike McCray posted on Twitter what so many were thinking. "Kaepernick has given so many people a voice and courage to stand up for what we believe is right, just like the people who came before us and sacrificed so much for our freedom and for us to have a voice today."

Campaigning for Change

DoSomething.org is a national group of millions of young people who want to make a change in the world. Their actual motto is "DoSomething. org makes the world suck less." They sponsor a number of different campaigns to bring awareness to issues. To get involved, first go to the website (www.dosomething.org), sign up for a campaign, and create an account. Next find ways to get involved in the campaign, send in a picture and get the movement in motion. Some of the projects the group has done so far include donating five million pairs of jeans to homeless youth, teaching more than 11,000 older adults how to stay up-to-date on technology, cleaning up 3.7 million cigarette butts from the streets, and distributing 343,000 pairs of thumb socks to remind people not to text or talk on their phones while driving.

One of DoSomething's projects came in response to the June 17, 2015, murder of nine black people during a hate crime in Charleston, South Carolina. More than 26,000 people shared their thoughts on the website. In the site's virtual poetry slam, 7,690 members participated, and 3,394 poems were shared. One writer, Jordon, won a $3,000 scholarship for her poem. She stated, "The Mic Check Racism Campaign is important to me, because racism impacts people of ALL races. I am striving to make this world a better place for all of us human beings, and that cannot happen until we can learn to love and live in equality. So hopefully," she adds, "by participating in this campaign, I was able to open some people's eyes towards the damaging effects of racism, and teach them a valuable lesson!"

The Psychology of Racism

Racial inequality causes unhappiness and anger, but it can also damage a person's physical and mental health. In fact, in some health circles, racism is considered a serious public health issue. According to a number of studies, black people who experience racial stress as teens are far more likely to develop chronic diseases in adulthood, including high blood pressure, higher body mass index (BMI), and higher levels of stress hormones. It does not take obvious discrimination to cause these health issues either. Just fearing that discrimination will happen is enough to trigger a rise in blood pressure, and cause your body to experience stress.

Exposure to ongoing anxiety, such as racial bias, can even change the structure of the brain, according to a recent study published in *Molecular Psychiatry*. Chronic stress increases the growth of some brain

Discrimination and prejudice are not only emotionally stressful. They can even impact your health in various ways.

cells and inhibits the development of others. Experts believe this can result in long-term and possibly even permanent changes to the brain in the areas of learning and memory.

It is crucial to recognize the toxicity that arises from racial inequality, says April D. Thames, assistant professor at the University of California Los Angeles. She states, "Hence, it is time for scientists, mental health professionals, and policy-makers to 'Stand Our Ground' and deal with the toxicity of racial inequality that not only impacts the individual, but society as a whole. These are critical issues that we simply cannot ignore, or hope that they will somehow disappear."

Another connection between racism and overall health was discovered in a study from the Slone Epidemiology Center. It showed that, of the 38,142 African-American women it followed, the more discrimination they encountered, the higher the risk of developing adult-onset asthma. Patricia Coogan, research professor and epidemiologist stated, "Racism is a significant stressor in the lives of African American women, and our results contribute to a growing body of evidence indicating that experiences of racism can have adverse effects on health."

Unconscious racial biases of doctors can also impact a person of color's health. In a 2012 report published in the *American Journal of Public Health*,

Depending on how often you encounter it, the issue of race may at first be barely noticeable, and then become progressively more of a nuisance. Annoyance can easily blossom into anger.

researchers found that doctors tend to spend less time with black patients than with whites, and this can end up making African-American patients feel unwelcome. When this attitude is coupled with a general lack of adequate health insurance coverage, it can result in blacks dying from a variety of diseases at higher rates than other racial groups.

Living with racism does more than stress the body; it also stresses the mind. A 2014 study published by the American Academy of Pediatrics, interviewed 1,170 young people of color between thirteen and seventeen years old. The research revealed that 85 percent of these teens had experienced racial discrimination, and they had a higher likelihood of developing major depression, anxiety, and social phobia. Lead author of the study, Lee M. Pachter, stated, "Sixty years after *Brown v Board of Education*, racism remains a toxic stressor commonly experienced by youth of color."

A study done in 2016 at Manchester University supported these findings. It explored how racial attacks, such as being shouted at, being physically attacked, avoiding a place, or feeling unsafe because of ethnicity, impact a person's mental and physical health. The study was published in the *American Journal of Public Health*. Lead scientist Dr. Laia Becares said, "Our research highlights just how harmful racial discrimination is for the health of ethnic minorities. We see how the more racism ethnic minority people experience, the more psychological distress they suffer from."

Racism is a negative experience for everyone, and it can truly damage one's mental and physical health. While stopping racial inequality is not something that any single person can do, finding ways to cope with it and changing how it affects your life is within your control. Time to start making some plans.

CHAPTER FOUR

Coping, Healing, and Moving Forward

Many readers will be familiar with the ways racial inequality makes them feel. They may notice it around them and be dismayed, even if they are not its victims. Others may have grown up knowing they are part of a minority that has been disenfranchised. Perhaps they have suffered the nicknames and the slurs, and been misunderstood or mistreated. The threat of violence against them because of their appearance and identity can be very real, and even an everyday occurrence.

Unfortunately, it will probably be a long time before any or all forms of racial inequality are wiped out in our society. The best you can do—especially if you are a person of color—is to arm yourself with knowledge and develop the coping skills to keep yourself sane, and to maintain your self-respect and self-esteem. Taking care of yourself is essential, so know what you need to do to keep yourself healthy and strong.

Tiny Indignities

You may not have been the victim of loud, overt racism, but chances are you might have experienced what the experts call microaggressions. This term was first used by psychiatrist Dr. Chester Pierce in the 1970s and then later expanded upon by psychologist Dr. Derald Wing Sue at Columbia University. Microaggressions are what are known as unintended discrimination. Dr. Sue defined them as "brief and commonplace daily, verbal, behavioral, or environmental indignities, whether intentional or unintentional, that communicate hostile, derogatory, or negative racial slights and insults towards people of color." These actions or comments are often subtle and they unintentionally or unconsciously reinforce negative racial stereotypes. Some examples include a white girl tightening her hold on her purse when a Latino person walks nearby, an Asian American being complimented for speaking "such good English", a black couple being seated near the

Different people may have different perspectives on the same experience. For example, a diverse collection of students in a dorm meeting may all have different ideas of what "offensive" means.

kitchen in a restaurant even though there are better tables available, or a Native American being told, "Wow, I don't even think of you as an Indian".

It is likely that, most of the time, microaggressions are not meant to be insulting, yet they can certainly feel demeaning under certain circumstances. So, how do you handle them? Recognize that you're not being overly sensitive. Feeling hurt or angry is normal. You might be able to let it go, especially if you really like the person who made the comment. You can just choose to walk away from the moment.

Other times, the experience may fester like a wound and that's when you need to take some action. As psychologist Ellen Hendrikson writes online, "Trust yourself. If the comment sticks with you, even hours later, or it makes you mad or sad to replay in your head what happened, know you don't have to swallow it like a hot coal. Tell someone," she continues. "Talk to

If you are close to someone, you may feel you share enough as friends to challenge them on something racially inappropriate they may have said or done. This can even help improve your friendship.

someone who gets it, no matter their color." Find a friend, parent, relative, teacher, or other trusted adult and explain how you feel.

Another way to respond to microaggressions is to take a minute and ask the person, "What did you mean by that comment?" Often this question is enough to make the person more aware of what he or she has just said. You might also try saying, "That comment was pretty offensive to Hispanics" or "You know, comments like might be upsetting to blacks." You might even personalize the statement and say, "It hurts my feelings when people say those things, because . . ."

These are fairly gentle ways of teaching an important lesson. Speaking honestly and tactfully is often the key to getting through to others. If you let your frustration guide you, your words may come out angry and that can elicit defensiveness in the other person. If that happens, the lesson will most likely be lost, and a relationship may end.

Racist Terms

When Republican National Committee Chairman Michael Steele used the term "honest injun" in one of his speeches, it was not take long before he found himself in big trouble. The Native American community quickly let him know that was a term they did not care for. It had been used for years to insult different Indian tribes. Are there other racist terms that are in everyday vocabulary that could be considered offensive? You bet.

Boy: This is a normal word when applied to a young male of any background, but when used to refer to an adult black male, it is a problem. Since racists generally see black people as inferior, the term "boy" has been used to insult them.

Thug: This word refers to a particularly violent or aggressive person, especially a criminal. It has been used to refer to violent people of all ethnicities. But many people nowadays have added a certain amount of sting to the word, because they have used it as a code word for black person. Many activists and educators consider it a thinly veiled version of the n-word. It is also an example of what many observers have termed a "dog whistle." It is a word that is intended to convey a meaning to a certain group of people, while being ignored by others—the way a dog whistle's pitch can only be heard by dogs, hence the name.

Indian giver: Although the actual meaning of this term has not been established, a number of people believe it refers to someone who gives a gift and then demands it be given back. It was an insult to Native Americans and is still considered insulting.

Gypped: This term is usually used to indicate that someone has been cheated or conned. It comes from the word gypsy, the Roma people were often stereotyped as thieves or tricksters.

A Bigger Problem

It is one problem when you are coping with racist behavior from friends or classmates. But what happens if it is coming from a teacher or other faculty member at your school? Current statistics show that about 80 percent of the country's school teachers are white. This can cause racial issues in a number of classrooms.

If you believe a teacher is treating you differently because of your race, be sure to write down all the details you possibly can. Exactly what happened and when? What was said and by whom? Did anyone else witness it? Take this information to your parents or other trusted adult. Ask to see your school's policies

A good teacher will make an effort to include all students in class activities and discussion, including students of all backgrounds and levels of accomplishment.

on racism. Finally, contact the school administrator and determine who the information should be taken to. With your parents or other adults, present your evidence factually and clearly. Hopefully the school will investigate what is happening and you will either see immediate changes—or a different teacher in the front of the classroom.

Staying Cool and Calm

Multiple studies have made it clear that ongoing stress is hard on your emotional, mental, and physical health. Keeping your stress levels down is truly important. It will not only make you a calmer and healthier person, but it will make it easier to make the best decisions on how to deal with any racial issues you encounter. How can you help keep your stress levels down? Here are a few ideas to try:

• Surround yourself with a strong support system of friends and family. These people love you and are typically willing to do whatever you need—from giving you a great big hug to lending an ear when you need to vent.

• Join any possible student associations for people of color. Being around like minded people can make everything easier because they understand exactly what you are going through and often have great advice and suggestions.

• Take care of your body. This means doing the things your parents keep telling you to do—get enough sleep at night, exercise, and eat healthy food. Physical activity is a great way to release stress, but do not push yourself to do something you do not enjoy. If you hate running, don't focus on jogging. There are many fun ways to get exercise, including skateboarding, hiking, biking, or swimming.

• Spend time doing what you enjoy most. No matter how busy you are, find a way to make time

Blowing off steam by doing physical activities—whether that means joining a team or just jogging with friends after school—can reduce stress and anxiety.

for whatever hobbies you like to do. Being creative is a great way to relax and feel better about yourself and the world.

• Read supportive and helpful books and other resources. Check out your local library and see what kind of materials they might have about racial inequality and how to deal with it. Ask if there are any support groups or upcoming programs geared to the topic. (If there aren't, now is the time for you to suggest that changes!).

• Meditate, get outside, or do some deep breathing. All of these activities will help your body and mind relax.

• Practice positive affirmations. Since racism commonly attacks a person's overall self-esteem, taking time to bolster it with some positive affirmations can be helpful. Some helpful ones to try include: I love and accept myself unconditionally; I approve of myself and feel great about myself; I am a unique and very special person and am worthy of respect from others; and it matters little what others say, what matters is how I react and what I believe.

Seeking Help

What happens when you meditate, sleep well, read books, and talk to your friends and it still isn't enough?

Therapy and counseling are not only for students with diagnosed disorders. They are also recommended as ways to prevent and manage the stress that anyone can experience.

It might be time to seek out the guidance and help of a professional. You could start with your school's counselor, or you can try to talk to your parents about seeing a certified therapist, psychiatrist, or psychologist. These experts can help you explore your feelings, plus help you find the resources you need to cope with and control your stress levels.

Just being able to talk about your experiences is frequently a relief.

In addition to seeing a counselor of some type, you can also call one of the many hotlines available for teens struggling with various issues, including the impact of racial inequality, like Teenline at 310-855-HOPE and the National Suicide Hotline at 1-800-273-TALK.

What if you are not the one dealing directly with racism, but instead see it happening around you and want to affect some type of change? In a speech in Cleveland, Ohio, Margaret Mitchell, president and CEO of YWCA, encouraged everyone to get involved in ending racial inequality. As reported by the Not In Our Town website, she told her audience:

> *There is a cure against racism. The deep wounds can be healed but the healing process is intricate, deliberate and will require involvement from those who have previously*

By some accounts, the modern generation of young people is the most open to diversity and ready to combat the intolerance and anger that still plague race relations.

remained silent. When racism raises its ugly head, silence becomes toxic and our apathy is interpreted as total acceptance. We always have a choice: do nothing and let racism go uncontested and flourish, or do something—act up, rise up, and speak up. We must pick up the armor of righteousness daily in order to slay the evil forces of racism at work against us...It will not be easy and it will not always be comfortable for any of us but courage is a game changer. We must each take a step each day to garner support and find our voice as the moral majority.

In order to act up, rise up, and speak up, as Mitchell recommended, people must make changes. Learn about other cultures and explore what you don't know much about. Think before you speak, and be a role model to others. Always remembers that stereotypes tend to be harmful and never assume, because, chances are, you will be wrong.

10 Great Questions to Ask a Counselor

1. How can I respond to racial insults or treatment?

2. What is the best way to handle it when someone tells a racial joke?

3. Where can I turn for help if I am threatened or feel as if I'm in danger?

4. What resources are available locally to support me?

5. What books can I read that explain racial inequality?

6. What should I know about my civil rights when interacting with police officers and other authorities?

7. How can I educate myself about cultures other than my own?

8. What can I do to ensure I have the same educational opportunities as every other student?

9. How can I stand up for people of color if I am not a person of color?

10. How can I talk to my peers or family if they are clearly racist in their behavior?

CHAPTER FIVE

Be Bold and Brave

Recognizing racial inequality in all its forms comes first. Responding to it effectively comes second. Coping in healthy ways is third, and then, at last, is translating these experiences into something positive. When responding to inequality leads to empowerment and helping yourself as well as others, you are definitely the winner.

Now that you are more aware of racism and its impact on you, on your life, and on your community and world as a whole, it's time to do something about it. Attending any local support groups is a great step, and organizing a group if one does not exist is a terrific step to make. Your involvement does not need to stop there, though.

Getting Organized

If you attend a school or live in a city that already has an active social justice group like Black Lives Matter, an immigration reform activist collective, or other organization geared for people of color, reach out to them and see how you can get involved. However, if you find your area is lacking such a group, don't give up. This is your chance to start your own group.

If possible, start by searching out a few like-minded people to help share the work with you. Once you have a friend or two who are interested in helping, decide on a tentative name for your group and take time to write out your mission. Ask what you want to achieve and why, and then figure out how you will do it. Are you focusing on anti-racist activities, immigration reform, or another topic? Set some goals and don't hesitate to share the effort with other members.

Next, choose a location for your meetings. It should be one that is easy to find and can accommodate all your members. (Make sure you have permission to use the space on a regular basis). Once you have all of these steps in place, it's time to do some advertising. Put up flyers around school and see if you can put information or write articles about your

(continued on the next page)

Organizing a group can sound intimidating, but even just a group of friends meeting after school in a park can start a group. All it takes is a few like-minded people who want to make a change.

(continued from the previous page)

group in the school's newspaper or web site. Create posters and post them in high traffic areas like the school library or cafeteria. Ask if you can put them up in nearby coffee shops, bookstores, and other places students tend to frequent.

Another obvious and easy way to drum up attention and attract members is via social media. On a platform like Twitter, you can hastag #BLM and your community's name together, or your school, church, or other groups that may be sympathetic to the cause. On Facebook, set up an event to introduce people to each other. You can make it a closed or open group, depending on who you want to reach, and how private you might initially want to make it.

The great thing about building a group from the ground up is that you and whomever you partner with can organize it exactly how you want. Making the rules and figuring out what you want to do and how to do it are not only great ways to make a difference, but they are also great learning experiences. Many activists and organizers started this way in their teens, adhering to a "Do-it-yourself" philosophy, or DIY for short.

Once you have your group together, now what? Some of the activities you can organize with your group include panel discussions, film showings, informational pickets, outdoor rallies, information tables, and field trips to civil rights sites.

Peaceful Protest

Protesting against injustice and inequality is important, but should be nonviolent. Mohandas Gandhi agreed. "We are constantly being astonished these days at the amazing discoveries in the field of violence," he stated. "But I maintain that far more undreamt of and seemingly impossible discoveries will be made in the field of nonviolence."

Peaceful protests are often a wonderful way to bring awareness to issues. They send a strong message but in a way that does not involve anyone getting hurt or feeling threatened. The sit-ins at lunch counters a half century ago are an excellent example. Today's Kaepernick Effect is another one. According to the King Center, Martin Luther King Jr. once said, "He who passively accepts evil is as much involved in it as he who helps to perpetuate it. He who accepts evil without protesting against it is really cooperating with it."

Protesting can take many different forms. Sharing your message is always the primary goal. While skywriting or mass petitions might be beyond the scope of you or your group's budget and time, there are many other, smaller projects you can undertake. These include conducting local petitions; picketing or striking; occupying a public space; displaying banners and posters; holding candlelight vigils; singing; walking out; sponsoring sit-ins; encouraging consumer boycotts; making public speeches; writing letters of opposition or support to

Older teachers, professors, and former activists in your orbit may have advice for you when it comes to organizing, activism, and protest, including how to do it legally and safely, but effectively.

newspapers and other printed or online media sites; distributing leaflets, pamphlets, and other materials; wearing symbols; organizing parades or marches; and fasting or going on a hunger strike.

Although peaceful protests are just that—peaceful and nonviolent—always talk to your parents about participating in them first. They may have some advice, input, or precautions they want to share with you. The same may be true for teachers, faculty advisers, guidance counselors, or members of organizations in your area that have experience in these kinds of things.

You may be surprised by the degree of activism in your immediate social circles when you start asking around. There are many people who have and continue to be involved in activism, even if they don't seem like the type to be. Such people can help you learn the ropes, and serve as role models. They may also be able to point you to important works about organizing, including books about people's movements around the world.

You can look up groups online that are active in your city, town, or county. Thes may be grassroots organizations with only a few people. Think about how energized they might be to unite with your own group. They may even want you to join theirs, or vice versa. The possiblities are endless when you reach out in an earnest, heartfelt manner.

Giving Back, Mentoring Others

One way to give back to your peers and your community as a whole is to become a mentor for others. Although the definition of mentor changes from one person to the next, the overall meaning is a trusted advisor. A mentor is someone who is there to support you and advise you, always keeping what is best for you of paramount importance.

Pamela Ryckman, author of *Stiletto Network: Inside the Women's Power Circles that are Changing the Face of Business*, writes, "Mentors help fill your knowledge gaps and seek opportunities to help you grow and excel. A mentor is someone with whom you can let down your guard, share your insecurities, and ask the 'stupid' questions we all have sometimes."

As a mentor, you can help others struggling with a variety of racial issues. You can actively advise, coach, encourage, listen to, and support them. You can also help them access local resources, and act as a strong role model. By helping others, you make yourself stronger, and you make the world a better place. As Robert F. Kennedy stated, "Each time a man stands up for an ideal, or acts to improve the lot of others, or strikes out against injustice, he sends forth a tiny ripple of hope . . . building a current that can sweep down the mightiest walls of oppression and resistance."

Faith and the Legacy of Activism

Often, faith-based groups and organizations, including the clergy and sometimes congregations of churches, synagogues, mosques, and other houses of worship, are involved in all sorts of projects. Many work on human rights or anti-poverty campaigns, and even civil rights. You can attend services and try to meet people without having to compromise your own values, whether you are religious or not. Be open-minded and open-hearted in doing so. After all, part of fighting for racial equality involves recognizing that religious differences should also not be something that divides people in the quest for justice and equality.

Many of the most famous and world-changing movements for human and civil rights have arisen in communities of faith, and were directly or indirectly inspired by the faiths of important members of those struggles. Martin Luther King Jr., after all, was a Baptist minister. Mahatma Gandhi, whose leadership of a peaceful movement that helped liberate India from British rule, was influenced by many faiths besides his own Hinduism in his philosophy of nonviolence. Many members of the Quaker religious movement were influenced by their principles to become abolitionists, fighting against slavery in the nineteenth century.

Deciding to become active in anti-racism efforts means not only organizing and meeting up, but actively listening to what others tell you about their experiences, and sharing your own.

One thing that comes from meeting people of other faiths and ethnic groups is realizing that many people are more similar than they are different. Even those who seem like they have it all mave have been challenged in some way, or felt excluded. African Americans, Jews, Muslims, Christians, Hindus, and many others have much to learn from each others' experiences and struggles.

Today, the world is at your fingertips, making connecting and networking with others who share a desire for social change as simple as a few clicks of the mouse.

Social Media Do's and Don'ts

We live in a technological environment that the civil rights leaders of the past did not fully anticipate decades ago. The online world is normal and routine to you, but it would be mind-boggling to some of the biggest historical icons of activism. With just a couple clicks or swipes on keyboard or a screen, you have the ability to share a thought, send a message, post a photo, organize an event, or pose a question to the rest of the world. This makes promoting racial equality concepts, projects, and social movements so much faster. You can post on a social media site, write a blog post, record a podcast, or text a group a friends to gather together in mere minutes.

It is important, however, that you remember to stay safe when utilizing that technology. Protect your identity, as always. Do not reveal too much personal information to the cyber world. There are both internet predators and identity thieves who are more than happy to ignore your cause and take advantage of you.

A last word about inequality: be able to rise above race. Above all, we are human beings, and the color of our skin is as irrelevant as the color of our eyes, the size of our ear lobes, or if our belly buttons are 'innies' or 'outies.' If we work together, cooperate, and focus on what we all share, everyone, regardless of race, will benefit. A united society is one where each of us feels valued, respected, and free.

Glossary

advocate A person who supports a particular person, group, or cause.

affirmation A strong, positive statement.

assassination The murder of a political leader or other public figure, usually to make a political point.

civil disobedience Nonviolent protest used to challenge unfair laws or to voice other political discontent.

civil liberties Individual rights protected by law from unjust governmental or other interference, including the right not to be illegally searched, and rights to due process in court, among other liberties.

diversity The condition of having many different kinds of people in one's country, community, or establishment.

doctrine Ideas that are taught as truth.

dog whistle Refers to words or terminology that are used to convey hidden meanings to a certain audience, while keeping others ignorant of their true nature.

epidemiologist An expert in how patterns of disease develop.

en masse Together, in a large group.

icon A person or thing considered a symbol of something; for example, Martin Luther King Jr. is an icon of the civil rights movement.

indigenous Describes a people who come from a place, such as Native Americans.

internment camps Prison camps for confinement of political prisoners or prisoners of war.

microaggression An unintentional or intentional slight that subtly says something about another's opinion on race or identity that is less hurtful than blatant racism, but may sting nonetheless.

nonviolence A philosophy of protest and social change in which the participants pledge not to meet the violence of the state or authorities with violence of their own.

oppression The act of exercising cruel or unjust authority or power over people, including a specific sub-group of people like a religious minority or ethnicity, usually committed by a more powerful group, or the state itself.

POC Short for person of color, or people of color, a term used as shorthand when dealing with issues of identity, discrimination, and diversity.

slam Refers to a poetry slam, a competition in which poets read or recite original work.

segregation The enforced or even unofficial but noticeable separation of different racial, ethnic, or religious groups in a country, community, or establishment.

taunt To be challenged or yelled at in an insulting way.

unconscionable Not right, reasonable, morally or ethically defensible.

valedictorian The most accompished student in a graduating class.

For More Information

American Civil Liberties Union (ACLU)

125 Broad St. 18th Floor

New York, NY 10004

(212) 549-2500

Website: http://www.aclu.org

The American Civil Liberties Union (ACLU) is committed to defending the individual civil rights and liberties of Americans at all levels in the courts and within local, state, and federal government jurisdictions.

Canadian Anti-racism Education and
   Research Society

324-280 Nelson Street

Vancouver, BC V6B 2E2

Canada

Website: http://www.stopracism.ca

The Canadian Anti-racism Education and Research Society tracks hate groups and extremism in Canada, and lobbies government at all levels to initiate anti-racist policies and legislation.

National Association for the Advancement of Colored People (NAACP)

4805 Mount Hope Drive

Baltimore, MD 21215

(410) 580-5777

Website: http://www.naacp.org

The National Association for the Advancement of Colored People (NAACP) is one of the first ever civil rights advocacy organizations created in the United States, and continues to advocate for the rights of black Americans, and others who are disenfranchised.

Not in Our Town

The Working Group

PO Box 70232

Oakland, CA 94612

(510) 268-9675

Website: http://www.niot.org

Not In Our Town is a movement to stop hate, address bullying, and build safe, inclusive communities for all. Its films and other media, and its organizing tools, aim to help local leaders to build vibrant, diverse cities and towns.

Teen Line, Cedars-Sinai Medical Center

PO Box 48750

Los Angeles, CA 90048-0750

(310) 855-4673

Website: https://teenline.org

Teen Line is a nonprofit, community-based organization helping troubled teenagers address their problems. Its mission is to provide personal teen-to-teen education and support before problems become a crisis, using a national hotline, current technologies, and community outreach.

Websites

Because of the changing nature of internet links, Rosen Publishing has developed an online list of websites related to the subject of this book. This site is updated regularly. Please use this link to access the list:

http://www.rosenlinks.com/COP/inequality

For Further Reading

Aikins, Anne Marie. *Racism: Deal with It*. Toronto, ON: James Lorimer and Company, 2011.

Edwards, Sue Bradford and Duchess Harris, JD, PhD. *Black Lives Matter*. Edina, MN: Abdo Publishing, 2016.

Fremon, David. *The Jim Crow Laws and Racism in United States History*. New York, NY: Enslow Publishing, 2014.

Lentin, Alana. *Racism and Ethnic Discrimination*. New York, NY: Rosen Publishing, 2011.

Merino, Noel, Book Editor. *Racism* (Current Controversies). New York, NY: Greenhaven Press, 2009.

Parks, Peggy. *How Prevalent is Racism in Society?* San Diego, CA: Referencepoint Press, 2014.

Robson, David. *Racism* (Hot Topics). Farmington Hills, MI: Lucent Books, 2010.

Rodger, Marguerite. *Racism and Prejudice* (Straight Talk About). New York, NY: Crabtree Publishing Company, 2010.

Sanna, Ellyn. *We Shall All Be Free: Survivors of Racism*. Broomall, PA: Mason Crest, 2008.

Yuen, Nancy Wang. *Reel Inequality: Hollywood Actors and Racism*. New Brunswick, NJ: Rutgers University Press, 2016.

Bibliography

American Academy of Pediatrics. "Discrimination associated with mental health woes in black teens: Racism a Common 'Toxic Stressor.'" *ScienceDaily*, May 3, 2014. www.sciencedaily.com/releases/2014/05/140503082722.htm.

Associated Press. "Deputy Who Tossed a S.C. High School Student Won't Be Charged." *New York Times*, September 2, 2016. http://www.nytimes.com/2016/09/03/afternoonupdate/deputy-who-tossed-a-sc-high-school-student-wont-be-charged.html.

Bellware, Kim. "This is What Victory over the Dakota Access Pipeline at Standing Rock Looks Like." *Huffington Post*, December 4, 2016. http://www.huffingtonpost.com/entry/standing-rock-photos_us_5844c3b2e4b0c68e0481849f.

Bever, Lindsey. "School Officer Fired after Video Showed Him Body-Slamming a 12-Year-Old Girl." *Washington Post*, April 12, 2016. https://www.washingtonpost.com/news/education/wp/2016/04/11/school-officer-fired-after-video-showed-him-body-slamming-a-12-year-old-girl/?utm_term=.113d45b19bba.

Boston University Medical Center. "Experiences of Racism Linked to Adult-onset Asthma in African-American Women." *ScienceDaily*, August 15, 2013. www.*sciencedaily*.com/releases/2013/08/130815145153.htm.

Bruton, Dylan and Heather. Email interview with author. December 19, 2016.

Culp-Ressler, Tara. "Why Racism is a Public Health Issue." *ThinkProgress*, February 3, 2014. https://thinkprogress.org/why-racism-is-a-public-health-issue-b01056c63e44#.dq8rcednh.

Edwards, Sue Bradford and Duchess Harris, JD, PhD. *Black Lives Matter*. Minneapolis, MN: Abdo Publishing, 2016.

Ghandnoosh, Nazgol, PhD. "*Black Lives Matter*: Eliminating Racial Inequity in the Criminal Justice System." Sentencing Project, February 3, 2015. http://www.sentencingproject.org/publications/black-lives-matter-eliminating-racial-inequity-in-the-criminal-justice-system/#B.

Gibbs, Lindsay. "Tracking the Kaepernick Effect: The Anthem Protests are Spreading." *ThinkProgress*, November 3, 2016. https://thinkprogress.org/national-anthem-sports-protest-tracker-kaepernick-284ff1d1ab3e#.sznv2b7u2.

Goff, Phillip A., Ph.D, et al. "The Science of Justice: Race, Arrests, and Police Use of Force." Center for Policing Equity. Retrieved December 14, 2016. http://policingequity.org/wp-content/uploads/2016/07/CPE_SoJ_Race-Arrests-UoF_2016-07-08-1130.pdf.

Heine, Debra. "Obama Praises 'Outstanding Work' of Black Lives Matter Organizers at White House Meeting." PJ Media, February 19, 2016. https://pjmedia.com/trending/2016/02/19/obama-praises-outstanding-work-of-black-lives-matter-organizers-at-white-house-meeting.

Hendriksen, Ellen. PhD. "How to Deal with Racism." Quick and Dirty Tips, February 13, 2015. http://www.quickanddirtytips.com/health-fitness/mental-health/how-to-deal-with-racism.

Hsieh, Steven. "14 Disturbing Stats about Racial Inequality in American Public Schools." *The Nation*, March 21, 2014. https://www.thenation.com/article/14-disturbing-stats-about-racial-inequality-american-public-schools.

Ingraham, Christopher. "You Really Can Get Pulled Over for Driving While Black, Federal Statistics Show." *Washington Post*, September 9, 2014. https://www.washingtonpost.com/news/wonk/wp/2014/09/09/you-really-can-get-pulled-over-for-driving-while-black-federal-statistics-show/?utm_term=.111dfe002bbf.

Jackman, Tom. "This Study Found Race Matters in Police Shootings, but the Results May Surprise You." *Washington Post*, April 27, 2016. https://www.washingtonpost.com/news/true-crime/wp/2016/04/27/this-study-found-race-matters-in-police-shootings-but-the-results-may-

surprise-you/?hpid=hp_rhp-more-top-stories_
no-name:homepage/story&utm_term=.
ba02fb82ce1f.

Klein, Christopher. "10 Things You May Not Know
about Rosa Parks." History.com, February 4,
2013. http://www.history.com/news/10-things-
you-may-not-know-about-rosa-parks.

Lohmann, Raychelle C. MS, LPC. "Top 10 Stress
Busters for Teens." *Psychology Today*, November
19, 2014. https://www.psychologytoday.com/
blog/teen-angst/201411/top-10-stress-busters-
teens.

Luo, Michael. "An Open Letter to the Woman Who
Told My Family to Go Back to China." *New York
Times*, October 9, 2016. http://www.nytimes.
com/2016/10/10/nyregion/to-the-woman-
who-told-my-family-to-go-back-to-china.
html.

Manchester University. "Repeated experiences
of racism most damaging to mental health."
ScienceDaily, 26 July 2016. www.sciencedaily.
com/releases/2016/07/160726124047.htm.
Retrieved December 11, 2016.

Merino, Noel, Book Editor. Racism (*Current
Controversies*). Greenhaven Press, Farmington
Hills, MI: 2009.

"Mic Check Racism." Do Something.
Retrieved December 14, 2016. https://www.

dosomething.org/us/campaigns/mic-check-racism?source=node/709.

Miller, Ryan. "Black Lives Matter: A Primer on What It is and What It Stands For." *USA Today*, August 8, 2016. http://www.usatoday.com/story/news/nation/2016/07/11/black-lives-matter-what-what-stands/86963292.

Mitchell, Margart. "YMCA Greater Cleveland: 10 Steps towards Bridging our Painful Racial Divide." Not in Our Town, May 16, 2012. https://www.niot.org/blog/ywca-10-steps-toward-bridging-our-painful-racial-divide?gclid=CjwKEAiAp97 CBRDr2Oyl-faxqRMSJABx4kh9FfnnSkN-Nmj JqwSA2hgtpRMJUdGOCLJNeWfUbSaDTRoC Jkzw_wcB.

Nittle, Nadra Kareem. "The Top 5 Ways to Respond to a Racist Joke." Race Relations. Retrieved December 13, 2016. http://racerelations.about.com/od/takeaction/a/Five-Ways-To-Respond-To-A-Racist-Joke.htm.

Preciado, Caroline. Email interview with author. December 12, 2016.

Saeidi, Mahsa. "Bishop Gorman Football Player Suspended for National Anthem Protest." 13 Action News, November 22, 2016. http://www.ktnv.com/news/bishop-gorman-football-player-suspended-for-national-anthem-protest.

Sentencing Project. "Shadow Report to the United National on Racial Disparities in the United States Criminal Justice System." The Sentencing Project, August 31, 2013. http://www.sentencingproject.org/publications/shadow-report-to-the-united-nations-human-rights-committee-regarding-racial-disparities-in-the-united-states-criminal-justice-system.

Smith, Jacquelyn. "How to Be a Great Mentor." Forbes, May 17, 2013. http://www.forbes.com/sites/jacquelynsmith/2013/05/17/how-to-become-a-great-mentor/#54882710449e.

Stepler, Renee. "5 Key Takeaways about Views of Race and Inequality in America." Pew Research Center, June 27, 2016. http://www.pewresearch.org/fact-tank/2016/06/27/key-takeaways-race-and-inequality/.

Sue, Debra Wing, Ph.D. "Microaggressions: More than Just Race." *Psychology Today*, November 17, 2010. https://www.psychologytoday.com/blog/microaggressions-in-everyday-life/201011/microaggressions-more-just-race.

Thames, April D. "Toxic Exposure: The Impact of Racial Inequality on the Brain." Psychology Benefits Society, September 2, 2014. https://psychologybenefits.org/2014/09/02/toxic-exposure-the-impact-of-racial-inequality-on-the-brain/.

"The Rise and Fall of Jim Crow." OPB. Retrieved 11 Dec. 2016. http://www.pbs.org/wnet/jimcrow/voting_literacy.html.

"Unconscious Racial Bias among Doctors Linked to Poor Communication with Patients, Dissatisfaction with Care." Medical News Today, March 16, 2012. http://www.medicalnewstoday.com/releases/242975.php.

Worland, Justin. "What to Know about the Dakota Access Pipeline Protsts." *Time*, October 28, 2016. http://time.com/4548566/dakota-access-pipeline-standing-rock-sioux/.

YMCA, "On a Mission for Girls of Color: Inequality at School." Stand Against Racism.org. Retrieved December 14, 2016. http://standagainstracism.org/public/docs/inequality-at-school.pdf.

Index

I

Indian Citizenship Act, 17

J

Japanese internment camps, 19

K

Kaepernick, Colin, 49, 51, 53–54, 56, 86
King, Martin Luther, Jr., 23, 25, 26, 86, 90

L

Little Big Horn, Battle of, 17
Little Rock Nine, 21
lunch counter sit–ins, 23

M

Martin, Trayvon, 30, 31, 37

mentoring, 89
microaggressions, 65, 67, 69

N

National Anthem Protest, 47, 49–51, 54

P

Parks, Rosa, 21, 23
peaceful protest, 13, 86–88
Pearl Harbor, 19
Plessy v. Ferguson, 21
police
  bias against minorities, 41
  violence against minorities, 30, 33, 35
poll tax laws, 20, 26
positive affirmation, 76

R

race relations, in the United States,

About the Author

Tamra B. Orr has written extensively for readers of all ages. She graduated from Ball State University with a degree in education and English and has spent her life learning about the world. She and her family live in the Pacific Northwest, where she researches and writes during her work hours and goes camping and writes letters in her free time.

Photo Credits